THE IMAGINED GIFT

New poems of Lester Hirsh
begun in the month of
May of the year 2025

Imagined Gift- Credits

No portion of this book can be printed without written consent from Zen Napkin Press; and the author Lester Hirsh. Rules are applicable by law. **Copyright (C) 2025 Lester Hirsh.**

ISBN: 9781619180673

This book is an imprint of Zen Napkin Press. For more information contact lesterhirsh@hotmail.com or call 603-496-1186. Snail Mail correspondence is also encouraged by the author. 13 East Fourth Street, Watsontown, Pa. 17777-1201

All poems are original creations of the author Lester Hirsh. Any reference to other words of authors other than Lester Hirsh are acknowledged by quotations, direct, explicit, or obvious references made by Lester Hirsh in context of the poems. Epigraphs are acknowledged.

This book is published and printed in the United States. All rights reserved. First Edition.

Front Cover Art Work by Joseph McCann, Tampa Florida.
Inside Art- Street Parking; Universal Motifs; John's Pass; creations by my late friend and artist, Raquel Fruchter.
Other Inside Art- Solitude, by Nelly Zamora Jones
Man Leaning on Shadow- the Sketch beneath the last poem- Epilogue- by Lester Hirsh. quote-John Steinbeck- & Federico Garcia Lorca- Poem.
web sites: www.parisburg.beone.ws/lesterhirsh.htm
www.bignoisenow.com/hirsh.html

Other Offerings by Lester Hirsh

Books: *Photographs & Letters* (1982)- Mosaic II: Poems of An Ancient Order (1999)-
Sketchbook (2010)- *Lyrics of a Troubadour* (2013)- *Mexican Mosaics* (2014)-
Unpublished Books:- *Last Man Standing-Poems* (2015-2023) In *the Muted Wind* (2023-2024) *The Siren of Voices* (2024-2025)
Dangling Conversations (2025)
Albums: *Tales of a Troubadour* (1994) *Sweet Surrender* (1998) *Strangers or Lonesome Friends* (2003) *Lester Hirsh Live/Coffee & Tea Room* (2005)
Spoken Word CD- *Mosaic ii: Poems of An Ancient Order* (2005) Volumes I & II
Instrumental CDs:- *River of Strings* (2006) *Arpeggio* (2017) *The Other Side of Folk- Traditional Folk Ballads* (2015) *Fractured Suite-Live Tracks* (2019

Special Thanks to River Poet-Michael DeMarco, of Bloomsburg Pa, for The Imagined Gift transfer In Thumb Drive format, accomplished over cappuccino and friendly conversational discourse.

The Imagined Gift — Credits

This book is an imprint of Zen Napkin Press. For more information contact lesterhirsh@hotmail.com or call 603-496-1186. Snail Mail correspondence is also encouraged by the author. 13 East Fourth Street, Watsontown, Pa. 17777-1201

No portion of this book can be printed without written consent from Zen Napkin Press; and the author Lester Hirsh. Rules are applicable by law. Copyright 2025.

All poems are original creations of the author Lester Hirsh. Any reference to other words of authors other than Lester Hirsh are acknowledged by quotations, direct, explicit, or obvious references made by Lester Hirsh in context of the poems. Epigraphs are acknowledged.

This book is published and printed in the United States. All rights reserved. First Edition.

Front Cover Art Work by Joseph McCann, Tampa Florida.
Inside Art- Universal Motifs, a creation by my late friend and artist, Raquel Fruchter, as well as John's Pass.
Inside Art- *Solitude*, by Nelly Zamora Jones
Man Leaning on Shadow- the Sketch beneath the last poem- Epilogue-by Lester Hirsh. quote-John Steinbeck- & Federico Garcia Lorca- Poem
web sites: www.parisburg.beone.ws/lesterhirsh.htm
www.bignoisenow.com/hirsh.html

Dedication to the memories of Donald Hall and Jane Kenyon whose poetry and inspiration remain ever-present

Solitude / Nelly Zamora Jones

THE IMAGINED GIFT- TABLE OF CONTENT

Pebbles and Stones	13
Buddha in the Bookstore	14
Doing a Different Dance	16
When the Floodgates Open	17
When the Rain Had the Last Word	18
When Freight Trains Pass	19
The Imagined Gift	20
I Heard Geese Fly Overhead	21
Regardless of the Season	22
Failure to Launch	23
There Is No Telling	24
That Recurring Dream	25
Afterthought	26
Joining the Celebration	27
The Power of Persuasion	28
First Impression	29
In the Grand Scheme	30
Morning Meditation	31
Images at Dusk	32
Senryu	33
By the Clothesline and Beyond	34
Threading	36

Another Train Came Calling	37
In a Nutshell	38
Taking Time	39
In Light of the Keys	40
Self-Portrait in the Gallery	42
The Incomprehensible	43
A Short Chat with the Late Mary Oliver	44
Consolation	45
Anecdotal Evidence	46
In the Brief Company of Bill Moyers	47
What Some Seldom See	49
Of Time and Space	50
Beyond The Objective Correlative	51
Squirrels and Humans	53
Dog Days of Summer	54
On Matters of the Heart	55
Nature Can Be Kind or Cruel	56
The Parallel Apocalypse	57
The Diaspora	58
Universal Motifs	60
On a Day Off the Road	62
Epilogue	64
Author	65

No man really knows about other human beings. The best he can do is suppose that they are like himself.

John Steinbeck

The poem
The song
The picture
Is only water
Drawn from the well
Of the people
And it should be given back
To them in a cup of beauty
And in drinking,
Understand themselves.

    --Federico Garcia Lorca
     20th century poet/playwright

Street Parking / Raquel Fruchter

Pebbles and Stones

He launches a thousand memories
steeped in the past
drifting like a balloon
in the whim of the wind

A cartographer mapping out
the serpentine course of his life
he picks pieces apart
to no avail

One would think it best
if he could give up the ghost
and get on with what's left
of his life

but he prefers to sift through
fabrications, mother-of-pearl
shells from the sea
of his imagination

that upon closer scrutiny
turn out to be nothing more
than pebbles and stones that long ago
settled in the sandy sediment

Buddha in the Bookstore

He sits on a wooden chair
by the round table
at the far end of the bookstore.

He stares discretely at a young
slant-eyed gal with long black hair
using her thumbs to text message
someone on the receiving end
of the cell phone.

Suddenly she stops texting,
puts a piece of gum in her mouth,
picks up her purse and phone
and heads toward the front foyer
of the store to peruse other books.

In the meantime, the Buddha,
stares at the gray sky and cars
passing on a mid-morning
spring day.

Two other women sit by the bay window
in the far corner of the café, flipping pages
of magazines in a flippant manner.
The Buddha observes them as they
prepare to walk away.

He then ponders birds that congregate
in trees, and others that perch
on high wires chatting up a storm.

The Buddha takes pride in being a free thinker,
and has no explanation for the behavior of people,
then rubs his eyes with his fingers. To his surprise
in the interim, he has composed a poem about
what he observed before leaving the bookstore.

Doing a Different Dance

You can't compare the life you led
with those of others you know
more than assessing the value
of apples and oranges that fall
from different trees

Some folks have children
and others don't
we all do a different dance
in the transit of our journey

You may feel incomplete
but who is to say
you weren't meant to follow
the beat of a different drum

Be kind to yourself
you never know the sorrow
others feel or the emptiness
that may linger in their soul

You are where you are
they are where they are too
darkness can lurk behind
any door as light can enter in

It is best to wear
the shoe that fits
and get on with
whatever it is

When the Floodgates Open

Let the water rush

with memories of lost souls

lingering like sentimental post cards.

Grieve as you will,

but know the loved ones reached

their journey's end a bit before you.

Nothing you can do will bring them back.

Embrace the joy and sorrow

with a reverential forward

motion.

When the floodgates open

let the water rush

to the open sea,

where elements join

the nucleus of all life,

knowing memories remain

as long as you can hold them.

When the Rain Had the Last Word

It rained incessantly the day I drove
over two hours one way
for a mid-day performance.

The rain persisted like an infant
who cried and could not be calmed
by a doting mother doing her best
to cradle her infant with words and a pacifier.

Cars kept nudging me to speed up.
When I drove with caution they passed me.
Both the cars and drivers had an angry throttle.

On the way home rain followed me
like a detective with a tone of interrogation
raining on the window, the beat of a snare drum,
but more of an annoyance than a musical rhythm,
while the windshield wipers worked overtime.

The classical music station played a sad dirge.
I don't recall the composer but it was reminiscent
of a funeral march of all things, on a drab, dreary,
wet day. What else could be more unsettling.

I yawned most of the way home, doing my best
to stay awake and safe on the road. I pulled into
my pebbled driveway just before evening arrived,
tired, bedraggled, and drained.

By then, I was glad to be off the road,
and didn't care that the rain persisted. I was ready
to roll into bed and block out the bellow of an intermittent
downpour. That day, it was clear the rain had the last word.

When Freight Trains Pass

They come in the morning and night
with a rumble down the track
carrying freight on a fraught journey
few will ever know to where they go
or when they will arrive at their destination.

Graffiti on the rusted outer face
of the box cars are creative,
like murals often seen on the side of buildings
of any arbitrary city on the American landscape.

I hear the freight trains frequently
disturbing the morning silence,
like a boisterous John Philips Sousa march,
proud and intrusive as any spectacle.

This small town is otherwise demure,
except for cars and trucks
passing through downtown during the day,
but the rumble of trains, sometimes music to the ear,
are more often an annoyance than not,
as they lumber by at irregular hours,
sometimes as I sleep, or before I awake,
announcing themselves with a rattle
reminiscent of an underground tremor
that causes foundations of nearby houses to shimmy.

After a decade, I have grown used to the sound
of freight trains passing, perhaps as some folks
adjust to black flies in the country, but these trains
are not mindful of seasons, and keep coming
down the tracks unannounced and often.

The Imagined Gift

Titian, the Renaissance painter,
produced masterworks into his twilight years.
Picasso died in bed with his painter's palette
in hand.

What could be a more imagined gift
for a poet to be prolific and profound
until the very last breath.

The odds of achieving wealth
or universal recognition
might be as likely as finding gold
at the rainbow's end,

but the friend of fate
would be the valued work,
the poet, like the painter
before him,
knew his poems were sustaining
in the pinnacle of his imagination,
and the imagination of others
who would value his work
after he was gone.

I Heard Geese Fly Overhead

In the early morning
while still in bed
I heard geese fly overhead
on their flight to Canada
or some northern shore

in this latter part
of the mating season
that usually ends in early June

Their voices wafted
in the stream of air
for a moment or two
that I could hear

Then they were gone
in this early dawn
when the nascent
sound of silence

was interrupted again
by a passing car
on the street below

Regardless of the Season

The rabbit in the yard sifts through grass
creating a nest hole to protect
the coming birth of her kits

The spiders have spun
webs on the window
and in discrete corners
suitable to catch flies
and other prey

Bees are searching
for sunflowers, zinnias,
and purple lavender
to pollinate

I ponder the imminent arrival
of the summer solstice
and how swiftly seasons
come and go
in the circular cycle

thinking as much of darkness
as of light, and of shadows,
that are cast in the night

and of sadness
that has always been
a shy companion
regardless of the season

Failure to Launch

I've spent a life mired
in the illusion
that playing it safe
would deter me from
the embarrassment of failure,

while others
immersed themselves
in the frivolity of love,
just because, at the time
it felt like the right thing to do.

Those incurable romantics,
the Romeo and Juliet's
of their gilded age, who lived,
loved, lost, and
loved again, while I had
a failure to launch
beyond the safe haven
of the harbor.

Now that I'm old,
aching in the heart
and elsewhere, the thought
of rewriting the script
is still circumspect but welcome,
before time runs out.

There Is No Telling

There is no telling
how long the heat wave will last
or whether we will rise
the next morning
to greet the day
if sun or rain prevail

Life is not a given
any more than the worm
in the soil will evade
the hungry beak of a bird

It is fortuitous
to get on with the hour
like a carpenter who hammers
nails on the roof of his house
or the artist who paints
with blind passion
on his canvas

There is no telling
how long the siren of time
will sound

to steal the moment
like the first sunrise seen
on the horizon

That Recurring Dream

Each time the notion repeats.

That I live somewhere other than

Where I do.

This time, I was back again

In coal country.

I had just bought a house.

A friend was helping me move in.

Then the neighbors showed up.

Noisy, intrusive, loud as roosters crowing.

I realized the foreboding of my decision.

That curtains could not contain,

The loud intrusive chatter.

I knew I had made a terrible mistake,

Being a first-time buyer.

Fortunately, it was just another

Recurring dream, and I awoke relieved-

On a half cloudy, Easter morning.

Afterthought

Those high school days were difficult enough
navigating through the social network
staring at girls with long hair
and shapely legs in the classroom.

Surprised when one of them
you were secretly sweet on,
returned a smile and you flinched
in shy embarrassment.

There were so many dynamics
to deal with in those days,
the sad refrains after Robert F. Kennedy
and Martin Luther King Junior were assassinated.

When there were riots on city streets,
the Vietnam War intensified,
and the draft lottery was shown on TV.

Wondering whether the Cold War
would turn nuclear, or if the United States
and Russia would commence with World War III.

Then there was the afterthought,
that you never went to the Senior Prom,
and stayed home reading The Catcher in the Rye,
identifying with the outcast character Holden Cauldfield.

Those high school days were difficult enough,
dealing with those dynamics after your father died
when you were fifteen, and felt like a lost sheep
who had gone astray from the flock in the field.

Joining the Celebration

Sometimes it is best to let go the heaviness
to bask in the lighter side of thought
to breathe a sigh of gratitude
for being alive

for making it through another night
to see the sunrise lift over the horizon
to distance oneself from darkness
others envelope

to listen to bluebirds commiserate
with each other like family
intent on preserving the common good
of their community

to ponder the sound of a brook
running downstream or ocean waves
churning toward the shore

Sometimes it is best to let
the happy song sing
as you join in the celebration
of just being alive

The Power of Persuasion

It was the scent of her perfume

and her smile

that kept him crawling through

the forest of his imagination

in the lucid dream

until he found the watering hole

to quench his thirst

in the den of desire

before he awoke

First Impression

Thunder preceded the rain that came down on the roof like falling nails. It lasted for a minute or two before transitioning to a soft steady drone. For some parallel reason I thought of a Chopin etude, the way a players hands strike the keyboard in a steady arch of white and black keys, running up and down the scale of notes like a spider weaving her web. The composition in harmonic unison pleasing to the discerning ear.

This was a first impression, pondering the composure of nature's voice in sync with its cycle between storm and calm, darkness and light, all of which are necessary for the continuum of life.

In the Grand Scheme

I try not to fuss over the small stuff
or the shallow mundane matters
many strive to attain: fame and fortune,
and the power of influence-

Shakespeare said it aptly
in his play Macbeth,
that life is just a walking shadow.

Writer David Hume summed up
our tenuous essence
when he wrote,
"The life of a man is of no greater
importance to the universe
than that of an oyster."

Of course, he said that in reference
to the belief at times suicide is justified
depending on the circumstance.

In the grand scheme of the universe,
we may as well be a walking shadow,
of no more importance than that
of an oyster, but why sweat

the cosmos, when we can create
our micro universe in a poem
and celebrate the birth
of an idea,
because it feels important
for that moment in time.

Morning Meditation

In the morning, he saw light from the sun
and it was good.
He heard birds sing in the garden
and it was also good.
He turned on the news and saw dissent
on the streets of Los Angeles, Chicago,
and New York, and it was not good to witness,
even from afar on the face of a flatscreen TV.

It was then he pondered if the miracle of prayer
could alter the minds of men
in positions of power whose intent is to
manipulate and control a mostly peaceful
protest with the strong arm of an authoritarian
to call in the National Guard and Marines to quell
any dissent with disregard to the Constitutional
rights of a people to protest unlawful seizures of citizens.

It was only morning and it was hard to say
what would transpire throughout the course of the day,
or whether or not his morning meditation
would make an iota of difference in the turbulent world,
though he prayed that it would anyway.

Images at Dusk

Eight days from the edge
of the summer solstice
he sees a thin trail of fading clouds
looking like outstretched arms,
or the snout of a swordfish sailing in the sky.

It is nearly nine in the evening
but he is miles removed on the prairie lands
of the southwest desert, in a time warp,
lodged in the 20th century.

He sees a Native American man
with long black hair in a braid,
staring over the edge of a far ridge,
like the Blackfoot Indian Chief on a Buffalo nickel,
and there's a red-tailed hawk by the side of the road
surveying a land the bird calls home.

He remembers the Southwest school
tour of towns he and his partner
performed at back in 1978 and 79.

He puts his hand to his chin
sitting in the swivel chair,
in the bedroom by the desk,
leaning over like Rodin's statue
The Thinker, and ponders

how time, like the night before him
has slipped into that reflective space,
where memories still reside
in a deep well of that oasis
in the desert of his past.

Senryu

Boy at water's edge

dipped the pail into the well

drank his fill of life

--

The light reflected

on the edge of his deep sleep

behind the curtain

--

He longed to kiss her

as they lay in the brass bed

it was just a dream

--

The rabbit dug holes

in the lawn of his back yard

soon the kits came out

By the Clothesline and Beyond

I used to watch my mother hang clothes
outside the bedroom porch on the second floor
looking toward Shenandoah Heights
in the summer time.

We had a washer in the basement
and there was also a coal bin there,
in the far corner where the mine worker came
to pour a ton of anthracite down a metal shoot,
about once a month in the winter,
so that my father could shovel enough coal
in the belly of the furnace to heat the house
each night through the cold season.

But at the time we didn't have a dryer
and clothes were hung on the rung
of the clothesline with a pulley,
and the rope that extended out
where the far end was fastened
on a joiner hook attached to the roof
of our garage.

I felt safe and secure there in the summer,
talking to my mother as she hung
clothes one by one with the wooden clothespins.
I was just a kid but now and then I'd have
a premonition, thinking long into the future
when my mother and father would be gone
and I would be on my own in the uncertain world.

I never told her I had these thoughts
or how sad I sometimes felt even in the summer
when the night was about to set in
and I thought about the sandman behind
the bedroom door, and of dreams that haunted me.
She knew I felt safer sleeping with a night light on.

But something about being on the porch where my mother
hung clothes outside the bedroom I shared with my brother
and talking to her about nothing in particular,
or later when we were in the kitchen
and she was preparing supper
peeling potatoes and I cleaned string beans
putting them in the light silver colander
with holes in that water passed through
that were then cooked and served
as the vegetable along with the potato
and brisket of beef,

when I was still small enough to sit on the ledge
by the window looking out on West Street,
was a time I held close to the heart
somehow sensing those moments
would slip away like a fleeting dream.

Now that those years have passed
and my parents are long gone,
there are still times when I dip back
into that sacred place and find myself
drifting, watching my mother hang clothes
in the midafternoon with her youngest boy
by her side, both of them bonding,
and just glad to keep each other company.

Threading

Holes in the toes of my socks
thread their way in the world
of which I live

One complication or the other
penetrate the politics of siblings
and the power of the purse
they leverage

It's the age- old story
as ancient as Adam and Eve
and the serpent who lures
them into temptation

It's the bargaining chip
to avoid humiliation
to bow my head
and show gratitude
for the work I do
and crumbs of remuneration
I earn in return

The resentment spreads
like a mine fire
that burns through
seams of coal
underground

Another Train Came Calling

In the pitch dark at 1:30 in the morning

the train rolled by with its familiar chug-a-lug

those steel wheels roaring down the track

This time it woke me from a deep sleep

and I was freed from the prison

of a dream

This morning the details of that dream

have escaped me but needless to say

it was Kafkaesque

in its darkness

The trains thunder was reassuring

in that half alpha state of consciousness

turning over depths of the dream

like flipping a hot pancake on a grill

then shutting down the dial on the stove

Sometimes the passing train interferes

with the sound of peace and quiet

but this time it came calling

like a saving grace

In a Nutshell

We are born, we live, then we die.

It is best to keep things in that order,

and remember a baby is born

with his tiny hands curled in a fist,

ready to swing at the nebulous universe,

in front of his nearly blind eyes.

An old man on the edge of his last breath

relinquishes what he can no longer

hold on too.

When he dies his hands lie open,

just the opposite of a baby

born into the world.

Taking Time

It might be time to restore

the inner fortress,

to think about thinking about nothing,

as a monk meditating,

in the lotus posture.

It might mean

to go down to the river,

to sit on a wooden swing,

to watch the river flow,

to listen to birds sing

from their perch on a cherry tree.

Taking time might mean

to sit in silence,

to let the weary mind

hum an old forgotten tune

you once sang when you were young.

In Light of the Keys

There were no more pleasing and peaceful moments than the times I drove on the overseas highway down to Key West Florida. In the quiet of the car with no radio on, just humming along taking in the sight of blue ocean, skipping over the stretch of keys, starting with Key Largo, Islamorada, Marathon, the seven- mile bridge, then Big Pine, the Lower Keys with Deer Key, and finally the arrival at the southernmost tip of Key West.

In my short sleeve shirt, with a ball cap on and sunglasses clipped over the prescription pair, I was always excited as a kid to arrive on the last island where I would made a ritual stop at the Hemingway Home and Museum at 907 Whitehead Street. There, the polydactyl conch cats live and roam on the premises and are named after 20th century movie stars and writers, from Zane Grey, Clark Gable, and Shirley Temple, to name a few. In the backyard there is even a cat cemetery with a headstone inscribed with the name Marlene Dietrich.

When you walk into the Hemingway House you see and sense the history in the home and that bygone era of the 1930's. Surrounded by books and pictures, with mementos in every room, and the back loft where Hemingway wrote on his Royal Quiet Deluxe typewriter. You could sense his spirit still present with second wife Pauline Pfeiffer, whose Uncle Gus bought the home as a gift for the couple. In the back bungalow or cottage, is the museum with Hemingway books, CD's, pictures and pens available for the ardent collector to purchase. There is usually at least one house cat sprawled comfortably on the front counter like a royal guard over the estate.

I would always stop at one of the cafes for lunch on Duval Street before heading back, skipping over the Keys like a rolling stone that gathers no moss. Back in the 1980's I attended a few literary conferences in Key West where I met some of the luminaries in the field, at the Elizabeth Bishop conference and Nature Writers where I had the privilege of meeting and chatting with Elaine Steinbeck, the third and final wife of author John Steinbeck. When I think back on those moments and my pilgrimages to the Keys, it puts me at peace, feeling free as a seagull flying by the light of the sun, taking refuge in the southern paradise, commiserating with their own kind on the Island they knew as their home too.

Self-Portrait in the Gallery

Thinking over the course of his journey
there was always something that caused him
consternation stepping over every stone on the path.

He seemed to be seeking a safety net where one didn't exist,
except when it came to his art, where he composed
at times, with abandon and total confidence.

It was the irony of ironies.

Some would say he feared his own shadow,
while others saw him as someone who was secure
being the center of attention, especially
when he painted those self portraits
that were mostly dark, gray and self- centered.

Perhaps it was his sense of feeling lost in love,
or the strictures of society that valued material success
over one's spiritual essence.

Pondering the portrait in the gallery
reminded him of elements of himself
he felt others never fully saw in his life,
more than a century and a half later.

The Incomprehensible

Innocent children, their mothers,
brothers, sisters, fathers, cousins,
are caught in a crossfire of war,
in the Middle East and elsewhere.

Those that dodge the bullets,
smell the stench of suffering and death,
feel the pangs of starvation and uncertainty,
for what tomorrow will bring.

The more fortunate few find shelter,
in mortar and brick buildings
that still stand or haven't completely
crumbled from the nearby bombing.
They are starving and thirsty too.

Then there are the hostages,
another casualty of the conflict,
held in underground caverns,
narrow tunnels where they mostly
lie in the dark eating stale bread,
drinking dirty water fit for rats
and other vermin, never knowing
when THEIR CAPTORS will beat them
like a punching bag.

The hostages hope for an end of hostilities,
a ceasefire, and exchange of prisoners.

Meanwhile, here at home,
over 6,000 miles removed from the war,
I feel awkward stepping on a wasp,
crawling on the rug, thinking I could get stung
if I don't intervene.

A Short Chat with the Late Mary Oliver

I know you suffered in childhood

the darkness of abuse and neglect,

yet you survived into adulthood

writing poetry as pristine and overflowing

as a cascade marching over

a waterfall

I wish I could revel in the beauty

of a blade of grass, the sunrise

and sunset, the aroma of pine woods,

of daffodils in bloom, or the bright

varied colors of hollyhocks

as you could

We must honor

the nature of our being

content with our deficits, or degree

of enthusiasm

Suffice it to say many of your poems

have been a catalyst for my own,

even if the brush strokes created

on my canvas,

show more shadow than light

Consolation

I may never see these poems in print

but that can't deter the urgency

they have to be born

like a son or daughter

to come into this world

with hope to someday send

a ripple, however small,

to heal an aching heart

or inspire some searching soul

for words like these that might

console them in a moment of need

Anecdotal Evidence

Sometimes the fictions we create

seem more real than facts at hand

be it the hyperbole of gossip

or any other loose cannon

yet anecdotal evidence parses

in the politics of deception

to disguise an affair

that would otherwise do damage

In the end it might be wise

to let truth be the judge

of whether an honest take

leads to harmony or division

and let the anecdotal evidence

remain in the realm of writing fiction

In the Brief Company of Bill Moyers

As a young man I first came upon Bill Moyers, 6 Part Series on PBS- Joseph Campbell and the Power of Myth. Campbell was regarded as an intellectual giant and known to be a friend and confidant of novelist John Steinbeck. At the time, wrestling to cultivate ideas of my own in a fashionable manner of poetry and song, were challenge enough. To understand the complexity of Joseph Campbell and The Power of Myth, was for me, as difficult a proposition as reading Robert Bly's Iron John, a book about Men, adapted from the character of a Brothers Grimm fairy tale. I read Iron John and was perplexed with the weave of story, metaphor, and symbolism.

I didn't know much about Bill Moyers, or his serving as President Lyndon Johnson's Press Secretary, or his varied roles as a political commentator or journalist, nor his interests in religion, literature, philosophy, or science. I was unaware of the fact he was a prolific writer who would publish 42 books in his lifetime. As chance would have it that I once met Robert Bly after he gave a concert with a New World Reggae group as he choreographed and read his poetry at an MIT campus auditorium in Cambridge Massachusetts, I also met Bill Moyers at a Town Hall near Wilmot, New Hampshire where Moyers came to film and interview poets Donald Hall and Jane Kenyon for a documentary, A life Together: Poets Donald Hall and Jane Kenyon, in 1993.

On a short break between readings, the hundred or more folk in the community who crowded into the Hall for this historical event, walked out on a summer lawn for the intermission. It was there, I briefly encountered Bill Moyers who was alone, and probably about 60 years of age at the time. I made light conversation with him as he dragged hungrily on a cigarette. I found this to be most intriguing, thinking this wise holistic man would be the last person I'd suspect of being addicted to smoking. But then all of us, have some deficit we deal with, be it an addiction, or shy reserve, or insecurity we spend a lifetime doing our best to overcome.

Sometime later, I bought a copy of Moyers, The Language of Life, A Festival of Poets, in which he interviewed 42 distinguished, revered, luminary poets, including New Hampshire's Donald Hall and Jane Kenyon. I sit and read a number of these thoughtful interviews from time to time as other people of a religious persuasion would read a passage out of their bible for sustenance. Learning about Bill Moyers passing brought me back to the fold of memories, meeting him as he smoked by the branches of a lone tree. I also reflected on Robert Bly, who I approached after the concert at The Institute of Technology, and told him we had a mutual friend in poet Donald Hall. Bly asked me what my name was twice, then stared at me with his beady eyes and audaciously long strands of white hair, repeating as if in a chant- Lester Hirsh, Lester Hirsh, as I turned to leave the stage and wave goodbye to the poet and performer who wrote Iron John.

What Some Seldom See

Donald Hall once asked me in a letter exchange,

if I rewrote my poems.

I replied, sometimes as many as twenty times.

Donald replied to me, he sometimes rewrote

a poem as many as one hundred times.

We were both obsessed with the thought

of touching the talons of perfection,

if possible.

Donald was relentless in his quest.

I was too, but perhaps just a little less.

Of Time and Space

Physicists continue to modify their ideas of the universe, the gravity of black holes, quantum theories, the expanding or contracting realm of space, or how many billions of years back in time, the Big Bang occurred.

Closer to our modern era, the Rosicrucian's pursued inner wisdom through intuition, and visualization, believing in the interconnectedness of all things. Some historians claim our Founding Fathers, namely Benjamin Franklin, Thomas Jefferson, and George Washington had Rosicrucian leanings.

I find it just as enigmatic to observe the interaction and energy exchange between humans, and the intuitive power of animals who rely on that innate force of nature, to fend for themselves and survive in the Wilds.

It's a more pliable proposition for many to deal with the gravity of their own lives, in the minuscule world they do their walkabout, or in the expansive or contractive realms of fiction they create, or the dynamics of relationships with men or women they are drawn too, in this best of possible worlds Voltaire satirized in his novella Candide.

It would seem that is challenge enough for one swiftly fleeting lifetime.

Beyond The Objective Correlative

T.S. Eliot used it in The Waste Land
to describe a bleak and barren landscape
and dried up river.

Hemingway followed suit in his story
A Clean Well-Lighted Place, describing
the dark emotions of an old man at the bar,
who the week before, tried to commit suicide.

The description speaks to the reader,
rather than the writer in the first person
narrating.

The objective correlative in The Wasteland,
conveys that sense of spiritual decay and
disillusionment, soldiers felt
when they returned from the trenches
and horrors of World War I.

Hemingway used the technique describing
constant rain in *A Farewell to Arms*.
Erich Maria Remarque, brought the reader into the fold
of the trenches in his novel-All Quiet on the Western Front.
George Orwell in a similar vein in his- Homage to Catalonia.
Dalton Trumbo, in his heart-rending-Johnny Got His Gun.

The Objective Correlative may be a descriptive technique credited to T.S. Eliot and has become an effective writing tool, but the sad reality beyond it, is the real price suffered by soldiers and writers who witnessed and survived the horrors of war and collateral damage as a result of the exposure. They returned to civilian life traumatized in spirit and body, adorning Purple Hearts or other Medals, never quite the way they were before the war.

Squirrels and Humans

I'm impressed with the way squirrels
store their food, both hoarding and hiding
their bounty in several locations.

Humans, on the other hand,
buy their food in grocery stores,
bring their bags home, put perishables
in the refrigerator, hide the rest in cabinets.

We later cook meals for the family,
or, if we are single, sit alone at the table,
eating what we prepared for ourselves.

Squirrels hide their stash like misers
do their money, close to their nests,
and nurse their offspring on mother's milk
for ten to twelve weeks, after which the pups
forage for nuts, grains, and berries.

Perhaps the nuts and bolts of squirrel
and human habits are more similar after all.
We just forage on different turf.

Squirrels have to find their food
in the forest and fields, while we lazy humans,
simply drive to the convenient grocery store
where shelves are full of choices
to pick and choose, if we have enough money
to purchase what we want to eat later at home.

Dog Days of Summer

Why wait until August when dog days come
in June or July, depending on the year.

Some people dream of these days
in the dire stretch of winter,
wanting a reprieve from the cold.

Then summer comes like a tsunami wave
of scorching heat, and people lie prostrate,
in the misery of their sweating discomfort.

Not to mention the irritation of
the locust invasion, like in biblical times,
those Pharaoh cicadas come back to hatch
nymphs from its eggs and live another
four to six weeks above ground.

I remember when they invaded the forests
in coal country, humming like a static radio
to attract mates, when I was just a kid.

So much for the nostalgia of summer
and dog days, as I dream of cooler climes
of autumn, when sad refrains begin anew.

On Matters of the Heart

Maybe your sadness dwells deep inside
because you lost the love of your life,
or someone who was a fixture
of your inner family circle.

People who you relied on as confidants
during the most difficult times,
when their voices were a source
to share or commiserate with,
when you felt most vulnerable.

It takes time to heal an open wound,
and while we hold onto memories
of sacred voices and souls
that have transitioned, there are
new memories to make and new souls
in the wide world of possibility to behold.

You just have to open your heart
like flowers blooming in the garden
wanting and needing to be nourished
by the light of the sun, and the water
they drink from the falling rain.

Nature Can Be Kind or Cruel

After a rainstorm the air sometimes smells
like burnt ash at a campfire, and sometimes
like the scent of pine trees in the forest.

I suppose it can smell bitter or sweet,
depending on the memory we attach to it,
like lavender soap a woman washes with
that lures a man into her lair.

All animals rely on their olfactory scent
to determine what draws them in,
or detracts them from danger or delight.

A modest rain can be cleansing
like a shower after a day sweating
in the humid summer heat.

In the eye of a storm
with swirling winds and river swells,
that destroy property and people's lives,
in flash floods, it is a sad reminder,
nature can be kind or cruel without warning.

The Parallel Apocalypse

Woody Allen once spoke to graduates stating
"Mankind faces a crossroads. One path leads
to despair and utter hopelessness. The other
leads to total extinction."

It made me ponder the parallel pose of the
Robert Frost poem, Fire and Ice. Essentially,
they are two faces of the same Existential
Universe.

In Fire and Ice, Frost considers his preference
for the end of days before him. He finds merit
with the argument, an end in Fire could be fine.
On the other hand, since the end is inevitable,
Ice would also suffice.

I would rather put off the matter and live life
in the present moment, one day at a time,
with wine and roses, song and dance,
and let the burden of the future define itself,
without my encouragement, one way or the other.

The Diaspora

Beyond the displacement of people
those victims of war
living in tent cities,
due to their unfortunate fate,
most people know their own diaspora
or disconnect from elements in their lives.

I don't disparage or make light
of dire suffering,
anymore than to ignore the homeless
living on streets of American,
or underground
in the subway system
of New York City.

There is extreme deprivation
from Darfur, in Western Sudan,
to the sandstorm desert regions of Syria,
The Gaza Strip, in the belly of the beast,
throughout the Middle East,
Afghanistan, Saharan countries in Africa,
Asia, North and South America,
Bulgaria, Romania, Greece,
The West Indies, Haiti in the Caribbean,
and elsewhere around the Globe.

The Scriptures say the Meek will
inherit the earth. If that prophesy
comes to pass, what fruits of labor
will sustain the downtrodden,
when the powers that be
control distributions of wealth,
and divisions of labor among
The Have and Have Nots

Universal Motifs

It would seem
Life, Liberty, and the Pursuit
of Happiness,
would be a given.

We need Air to Breathe.
Food, Water, Shelter,
and a modicum of Love
to survive and thrive.

Yet injustice, famine and war
have persisted among nations
since time immemorial,

and the saddest tragedy
is the loss of life, especially,
of children caught in the crossfire.

If only the Universal Motifs
could be realized
and embraced
by the Human Race,

this world would be
a better place to inhabit,
share and assimilate within,
regardless of Race, Creed,
or the seed of discontent
that longs for resolution
among the huddled masses.

Universal Motif/Raquel Fruchter

On a Day Off the Road

You would think there is all the time to lay back

and accomplish a host of chores

read at least one unread book on the bucket list

or begin it and finish a chapter or two

as you have procrastinated doing

for forty years since a friend in Florida

urged you to read Homers, THE ODYSSEY

now that you are finally six chapters in

but are wondering where and when

your next gig will materialize

and the nervous pulse of fleeting time

sidetracks you once more and turns

the time- honored day off the road

into a different form of denial

for the task or tasks at hand

waiting once more for you to get beyond

fiddling the fingers of anxiety

and at the very least conclude

it is best first to take that walk

down by the river, sit on a wooden swing

listen to the birds sing their songs and reflect on

the precious fact you are alive and able

to do that at this moment in time.

John's Pass / Raquel Fruchter

Epilogue

Think of the scene on the silver screen.
The last episode of the long running series
Mash. It was February 28th, 1983.

Hawkeye and Hot Lips embrace
with an intense long kiss,
that says more in its silence
than any words could convey.

It's the story of our lives,
with or without the girl in the scene.
It's the unwritten epilogue,
like a shooting star falling from the sky.

We are here for a moment in time,
then we are gone with the wind.

Man Leaning on Shadow | Lester Hirsh

Author

Lester Hirsh was born and raised in Pennsylvania. He has also resided in Florida and New Hampshire. Originally from Shenandoah, in Schuylkill County, he currently resides in Watsontown, Pennsylvania, a few blocks from the Susquehanna River. Over a span of nearly fifty years, he has dabbled with divergent professional paths, among them being a touring acoustic road musician, and a substitute teacher. For most of those years he has plied his craft as a singer-songwriter performer, with a passion for music, fine arts, and poetry in particular.

He was a 1997 Finalist in the Napa Valley Emerging Songwriter Contest, Napa Valley California, and a 2005 Grammy Nominee in the Best Spoken Word category, for selections from Mosaic ii, Poems of An Ancient Order. He has been a rostered touring musician for the New Hampshire State Council on the Arts, and years later for the Schuylkill County Council on the Arts, artist-in-education roster, in Pottsville, Pa. He has also been a concert producer, most significantly, The Summer Solstice Folk Festival, he produced, choreographed, and performed in, at the Sovereign Majestic Theatre, in downtown Pottsville, in 2007.

Having attended three colleges, first, Dade Junior College in Miami Florida, followed by the University of South Florida in Tampa Florida, and 18 years later, through a division of the University of New Hampshire, Manchester New Hampshire, he earned a Bachelor of General Studies Degree, with an emphasis on Literature.

Mr. Hirsh was the publisher and editor of Bone & Flesh literary magazine in Concord, New Hampshire, from 1988-2002. He has produced four previous books of poetry, lyrics, and sketches, as well as 9 CD compilations of original music, which includes 2 Spoken Word CD's. In addition, he produced one compilation CD- The Other Side of Folk, containing songs of other renowned songwriters, as well as two instrumental music CD's.

His poems have appeared in The Asheville Poetry Review; Signal; Coal City; Tabula Rasa; Word Fountain; The Weekly Avocet; Bone & Flesh; and The River Poet's Anthologies, Bloomsburg, Pa. The Imagined Gift, is his latest collection of poetry and prose pieces composed in the spring and summer of 2025.